KW-364-586

MANCHESTER UNITED
FOOTBALL CLUB
TM

UNITED™
SUPERSTARS

Virgin

First published in Great Britain in 1995 by
Manchester United Football Club plc
Old Trafford
Manchester
M16 0RA
in association with
Virgin Publishing Ltd.
332 Ladbroke Grove
London
W10 5AH

Copyright © 1995 Manchester United Football Club plc

This book is sold subject to the condition that it shall not, by way of trade or otherwise, be lent, sold, hired out or otherwise circulated without the publisher's prior consent in any form of binding or cover other than that in which it is published and without a similar condition including this condition being imposed on the subsequent purchaser.

A catalogue record for this book is available from the British Library.

ISBN 0 86369 914 6

Produced by Zone Ltd.

Photography: John Peters, Action Images, Allsport, Sportsview, Frank Spooner Pictures

Printed in Great Britain

Statistics contained within this book are correct up until August 19th 1995

Contents

The Boss

What a season. As Alex Ferguson pondered the twists and turns of his first 'barren' campaign in five years, the need to retain the panache, the swagger, but above all, the appetite that characterised his teams' achievements was not lost on him, of all people. But his summer sales landed him in the dock, and the need for shuttle diplomacy to prevent his most prized performer quitting only led to further public panic. Let's just check the guy's track record.

ALEX FERGUSON RELAXES AT HOME AND SHARES A JOKE AT THE OFFICE
FACING PAGE: THE VEXED FEATURES THAT GAVE RISE TO THE 'LAUGH-ALONG-A-FERGIE' CARICATURE

Breezing into his new workplace on November 6 1986 to declare "I will not be satisfied until the European Cup is back at Old Trafford," Alex Ferguson could not have set out his stall with more clarity.

If Lee Sharpe – one of the Scot's most astute acquisitions in nine years at the helm – represents a bargain (£180,000 from Torquay in 1988), then the £60,000 compensation deal struck by Martin Edwards with Aberdeen counterpart Dick Donald for Ron Atkinson's successor can only be regarded as one almighty steal.

For his part, after ten trophies in six years at Pittodrie and a summer guiding Scotland in

the Mexico World Cup, the United job amounted to "the pinnacle of my career", one taking the spry forward from Govan to Queens Park, St Johnstone, Dunfermline, Rangers, Falkirk and Ayr United. Prior to Aberdeen he managed East Sterling and St Mirren.

Thanks to the counsel of Jock Stein – the man responsible for the first European Cup won by a British side, with Celtic, in 1967, Fergie knew that should the offer ever come, then – unlike Jock, he would not spurn it. Having turned down Barcelona; Rangers, and declined to permanently take on the national side following Stein's tragic pitch-side death in 1986, fate decreed that Fergie now challenge the received wisdom that no manager could succeed on both sides of the border. Challenge it and confound it.

Though what he found was a world away from the Scottish scene he had come to dominate with then-assistant Archie Knox, certain parallels exist and Fergie's formula – founded on graft, more graft and a bit more graft on top of that – duly delivered cups, titles and European success... a chastening Champions' Cup record notwithstanding.

The club's Salford HQ, the Cliff, was to find the ground rules overhauled; players re-assessed and the long-term strategy to break the Merseyside monopoly, rather than that of Glasgow's Old Firm, drawn up. Something fundamental to the cause was a meritocracy the like of which not even Sir

Matt Busby had presided over. In a dressing room too prone to clique, excuse, lack of fitness and the suspicion of favouritism, the new manager set out to ensure his players got the right answer when they followed his bidding: "Make sure you can take a close look at every single individual in here and say 'I'm glad I've got him on my side,'."

Still in Liverpool's shadow and knocked out of the '88 Cup by Forest, Fergie resolved to dismantle the side, and before things would get better they would get much worse – a 5-1 derby defeat, flirtation with relegation and a Palace home reverse that saw the axe loom.

But top flight survival and an FA Cup triumph – ground out entirely away from home – galvanised a belief to be justified by the winning of the Cup Winners' Cup against Barcelona the following May. By now, Ferguson knew he had men big enough to win things – even though, just as at Aberdeen, they would rarely do it the easy way.

Since leaving behind Mcleish and Miller, "Players with character, who could influence things around them," Ferguson had coveted just such a rock-like partnership – and Bruce and Pallister laid the foundations at the heart of the Reds' defence for a serious, tenacious and miserly title challenge.

They both shared his fear of failure and overcame the anger that greeted the sale of Paul McGrath – whose physique and concentration never quite matched his ability. The midfield transfusion took longer to take effect, with Neil Webb found wanting after an unlucky start. Between them, Robson, Ince, Phelan and Darren Ferguson eventually emerged as the team's core before Keane and Butt got on board in style.

Equally, goals were never to flow with the regularity associated with champions – that is, until the myriad expressive talents of McClair, Hughes, Sharpe, Kanchelskis and Giggs found liberation in the presence of Eric Cantona. Jim Leighton (ex-Aberdeen) never overcame a personal crisis of confidence, opening the door for the messianic – if ageing – Sealey and then the best 'keeper in United history, Peter Schmeichel.

Irwin and Parker too played an invaluable part in breaking the 26-year title hoodoo – but what this collection of individuals proved above all was that Ferguson was the first manager to grasp the shift of English football from a team game to a squad game.

Gordon Strachan, part of the Dons team Fergie brought down to Martin Buchan's testimonial in 1982, was to reflect in a 1990 BBC Scotland documentary, *Team of the Decade*: "He taught youngsters good habits, which they stuck to, and made players think 'we'd better do it for this man or we'll be in trouble'." This credo endures.

Asked if Ferguson's secret was his loyalty, Cantona once replied "The secret of Alex Ferguson is Alex Ferguson himself." So, there is no secret; just a love of football in harmony with the unique Manchester United way.

The Summer of '95 was a harrowing one for the man thought the year before to be in complete control of his own destiny. The Ince, Hughes and Kanchelskis saga prompted criticism as harsh as anything from the dark days of 1989. For those seeking capitulation under fire, however, one thing that's characterised Ferguson's career is the refusal to surrender – and hey, there's a European Cup to win!

"A FORMULA FOUNDED ON GRAFT, MORE GRAFT AND A BIT MORE GRAFT ON TOP OF THAT DULY DELIVERED CUPS, TITLES AND EUROPEAN SUCCESS"

Backroom Boys

Here are Fergie's backroom boys and girls, the ones who get less glory – but more sleep. The latest estimate at United's total full-time staff has nudged over the 400 mark – too many to pay on time, let alone list! From the chief executive and colleagues in the boardroom and plc to Cathy and Marie on the switchboard at Reception... here's an incomplete guide.

NORMAN DAVIES (RIGHT) SHOWS YOUNG ALBERT THE ROPES IN ANTICIPATION OF ONE LAST SEASON

BRIAN KIDD (FAR RIGHT) – THE MAN WHO COULD ONE DAY INHERIT THE OLD TRAFFORD THRONE

Brian Kidd is the first point of contact with the players and responsible for much of the variation in training that players compare so favourably with their previous clubs. A scoring star of the '68 European Cup win, his career was to take in two caps for England; Arsenal, Everton, City and Bolton. After a stint in charge at Preston, he helped set up United's local talent dragnet with Nobby Stiles before finding promotion thrust upon him just in time for the victorious Rotterdam Cup Winners' Cup trip in '91. A more than able and trusted lieutenant, 'Kiddo' is favourite to take over when Fergie finally vacates the hot seat.

Jim Ryan is another former United player, who played on the wing under Busby in the late sixties. His top-flight management pedigree came courtesy of Luton Town, though he was callously given the sack in the dressing room when the Kenilworth Road outfit had just defied relegation on the last day of the season in 1991. This will be his fifth campaign as manager of United's reserve side, with whom he won the Pontins League in '94.

Eric Harrison has been described as the best coach at the best club in the land. As his job is to mould the first team players of the future, an awesome amount of responsibility lies in his safe hands. A player with Halifax, Hartlepool, Barrow and Stockport, Everton made him youth, then reserve coach before Ron Atkinson snapped him up for United in the summer of 1981. He has taken the youth side 'A' team to six titles in nine years and triumphed in two out of five FA Youth Cup Final appearances – in '92 and '95.

Paul McGuinness is the man who stepped into Pop Robson's shoes at United's centre of excellence after the latter's summer departure for Sunderland. He is the son of Wilf, whose own career was cut short by injury before he coached the World Cup-winning England side of '66 and briefly took over from Sir Matt Busby. Involved in the grooming of boys at the club with regard to the media since his own premature retirement, the job now facing Paul is an even bigger challenge than that of replacing McClair for United against Bury in his father's Gigg Lane Testimonial back in 1990 (0-0). It might prove more exciting, too...

Jimmy Curran has been part of the furniture since hanging up his boots after injury and commencing an extremely slow tour of the bootroom. His medical know-how, picked up along the way in 21 years' loyal service, is now invaluable to United's kids, and his silken singing voice (stage name: Jimmy Buchanan) has brightened up many a long coach journey.

Norman Davies is one season away from retirement. The popular ex-mechanic arrived in 1970, as a mini-bus driver, but now presides over the textiles warehouse that passes for United's kit and laundry opera-

tion. Old friend Albert Morgan is waiting in the wings, but will hope his job description does not include running the gauntlet – as Norman had to on that infamous Selhurst Park night as Eric Cantona's escort.

Alan Hodgkinson, ex-Sheffield United and England 'keeper, has coached 'freelance' at United for six years; he is also regularly required by Everton, Scotland and Rangers.

Physio Dave Fevre came to United from Wigan Rugby League Football Club in 1994, and is thus able to act as a spy in the camp... for avid Red and ex-Wigan scrum-half, Salford's Andy Gregory! Dave has Robert Swire to keep him company when plotting the purchase of something even more expensive and hi-tech than the Cybex machine of which he is so proud at the Cliff.

Secretary Ken Merrett took over from Les Olive in 1988, having joined in 1966 as a book-keeper and wages clerk. The lay-preacher has been a prime mover in the pastoral life of United's staff ever since – including the two visits of the BBC's *Songs of Praise* cameras to the Theatre of Dreams. John Boyers is club chaplain.

Danny McGregor was drafted into the Commercial department, which has since swelled beyond all recognition, back in 1985.

Ken Ramsden has been the complete all-rounder since his arrival back in 1960. Now assistant secretary with responsibility for press and public relations, he spent many years charged with the smooth running of the ticket office at Old Trafford. Kate Longbottom is now head honcho in the ticket office, having been appointed as a cashier back in 1986. Her team are in almost the same demand as Fergie's!

Mike Maxfield left the Membership office to run the fledgling museum (curated by Mark Wylie) and tour centre, which has now become a major South Manchester tourist attraction. His old boss, Barry Moorhouse, is a familiar face to travelling Reds, as his logistical skills have been tested to the full on various Euro trips since his appointment as Membership secretary in 1987. He has served United in various capacities since arriving 28 years ago – co-incidentally the same number at which he stopped ageing.

Francis McHugh, club doctor, is involved in the medicals United give new signings as well as matchday duties. He played a crucial role in the recovery of Lee Sharpe from viral meningitis in '92.

Maurice Watkins could be forgiven for describing himself as MUFC's reading expert – as the libel buck stops with him. But in his dual role of director/solicitor, he has come to play a key role in negotiations – be they contractual, disciplinary... or anything!

Les Kershaw replaced Tony Collins as chief scout in 1987, giving up an academic career at Manchester Metropolitan University to head up a 40-strong national network.

Programme editor Cliff Butler and assistant Andrew Bubeer share a publications 'wing' with the magazine team of Rachel Jervis, Adam Bostock and Emma Hughes next to the Megastore, whose staff threaten to outnumber the playing side any day now.

Groundsman Keith Kent and team won Groundsman of the Year last season and are looking for a repeat performance.

Besides champion secretarial support, there's MU Radio (Matt Proctor); catering; security (headed up by big Ned Kelly); the stewards and boys like Alan and Harold at the Cliff, who all keep the club ticking over in their own dedicated and unfussy way.

JIMMY CURRAN, AKA BUCHANAN (TOP); KEITH KENT (MIDDLE) AND ERIC HARRISON (LEFT)

Peter Schmeichel

Voted the world's best goalkeeper by the press following the 1992 European Championships, the intimidating and acrobatic performances of Peter also persuaded the Professional Footballers' Association electorate to plump for him in their Premiership side for '93 – the year after Tony Coton and the year before Tim Flowers – yet he cost Manchester United one eighth of their fees put together!

WHO CAN FORGET HIS REFLEX SAVE FROM DON HUTCHISON WHICH PRESERVED THREE POINTS AT ANFIELD IN UNITED'S FIRST PREMIERSHIP-WINNING CAMPAIGN?

Because he is so sensitive to the suggestion, the giant Dane is constantly referred to as "the German" in the dressing room... then again, he has every reason to resent being compared to opposition so resoundingly beaten by his beloved Denmark in Sweden three years ago.

A neighbour of Brucie, the way they conduct their on-field relationship makes you wonder about the opinions expressed over the garden fence. But the two have an undying regard for each other, born of the mutual respect only a trophy haul like that of United's can bring.

His crucial save count is into the dozens now, but who can forget his reflex save from Liverpool's Hutchison which preserved three points at Anfield in United's first Premiership-winning campaign in March, 1993?

Successor to the popular Sealey, Peter has been dropped by the Boss only once – in Camp Nou, when restrictions imposed by UEFA meant the English birth certificate of Walsh was preferred.

Schmikes' debut, in a Sir Matt Busby testimonial versus Jack Charlton's Ireland, saw the least welcome of omens - a mix-up with Parker leading to an own-goal. Sure enough, Peter's mistakes have been few and far between ever since.

PETER SCHMEICHEL
Goalkeeper

Birthplace:	Gladsaxe, Denmark
D.O.B:	18th November 1963
Height:	6'4"
Transferred from:	Brondby IF 6.8.91
Previous Club:	Brondby IF
United Debut:	17.8.91 vs Notts County
Full International	Denmark

PETER SCHMEICHEL
LEAGUE RECORD FOR UNITED

Season	Apps	Goals
1991-92	40	0
1992-93	42	0
1993-94	40	0
1994-95	32	0
Total	154	0

PETER SCHMEICHEL
INTERNATIONAL FOR DENMARK

Debut:	20.5.87 vs Greece
Appearances	78

THE GIANT DANE IS CONSTANTLY REFERRED TO AS "THE GERMAN" IN THE DRESSING ROOM

Neville Brothers

Football is no stranger to the phenomenon of sibling rivalry... the Blanchflowers and Charltons... even the Wallaces, of whom three played for Southampton against Sheffield Wednesday in 1988! Manchester United had Brian and Jimmy Greenhoff in the 1977 Cup-winning side, and before that the Buchan brothers shared a brief period together at Old Trafford. Now it's Gary and Phil's turn to battle it out – the race is on to score the first first-team goal!

RIGHT: GARY NEVILLE
FACING PAGE: PHILIP NEVILLE

Sons of the Commercial Manager at Bury FC – the one and only Neville Neville – these footballing brothers have displayed an appetite for the big time to rival that of their musical counterparts.

Although capped by Terry Venables at right-back against Japan and Brazil following his sound FA Cup Final display, Gary's favoured position is that of centre-half, where, as Alex Ferguson says, his lack of height is at least partially made up for by his organisation, tackling and distribution.

Brother Philip has successfully filled both full-back positions – and was not far from choosing cricket for a profession – his batting being good enough to warrant the suggestion that he may have some day joined his netball star twin sister and Gary in reaching full international status.

Gary provided a timely bonus for the side in a season when injuries to Parker and May, along with suspensions to himself and Steve Bruce caused constant disruption to the defence. His debut came, however, way back in September 1992 in the disappointing UEFA Cup 0-0 home draw with Moscow Torpedo; replacing Lee Martin and getting a full two minutes! In captaining United to the 1995 FA Youth Cup, Philip went one better than his brother, who won in 1992 under Simon Davies!

After a faultless 4th round FA Cup debut versus Wrexham won by the Reds 5-2, Philip was pitched into the lion's den just over a month later in the Maine Road derby and again looked like he'd been around for years in a 3-1 win.

The family were at last "united" in the first team against Sheffield Wednesday in May, Gary switching to centre-half as Philip came off the bench after 25 minutes.

PHIL NEVILLE
Defender

Birthplace:	Bury
D.O.B:	21st January 1977
Height:	5'10"
Signed Trainee:	5.7.93
Signed Professional:	1.6.94
United Debut:	11.2.95 vs Man City
League Record:	1994-95: 1(1)

GARY NEVILLE
Defender

Birthplace:	Bury
D.O.B:	18th February 1975
Height:	5'10"
Signed Trainee:	8.7.91
Signed Professional:	23.1.93
United Debut:	8.5.94 vs Coventry City
Full International:	England

GARY NEVILLE
LEAGUE RECORD FOR UNITED

Season	Apps	Goals
1993-94	1	0
1994-95	16(2)	0
Total	17(2)	0

GARY NEVILLE
INTERNATIONAL FOR ENGLAND

Debut:	3.6.95 vs Japan
Appearances	2
Goals	0

Denis Irwin

The times Denis Irwin has pulled Manchester United out of the fire are too numerous to mention, yet over a five-year period, the fact that he has missed under 20 first-team matches is testament not only to his flawless temperament and fitness, but also to the incredibly high levels of performance he can maintain no matter the opposition. A firm favourite with Fantasy League managers, Denis' actual current market value is beyond calculation.

FREE-KICKS AND, OCCASIONALLY, PENALTIES HAVE BUMPED UP HIS ALREADY IMMENSE CONTRIBUTION TO THE SIDE

A native of Cork, the introverted Denis does not appear to have kissed the blarney stone, though his exploits in the colours of United and Ireland more than do the talking for him.

Faced with the humiliation of a free transfer from Elland Road, the determination Denis displayed in making the grade across the Pennines at Oldham is just one reason Alex Ferguson plumped for him to fill the 'problem' right-back position after a succession of midfielders in the number 2 shirt had seen United through to a triumphant FA Cup-winning climax to season 1989/'90.

Having stood out in the side which came so close to knocking the Reds out in their replayed Maine Road semi, Irwin jumped on the United 'bus' with zest, and had a ECWC winners medal to show for his first season.

Now settled on the left, his fee, £650,000 (in an era of multi-million pound full-backs), looks like a bad joke – for Latics and Leeds (who tried buying him back in 1992) fans at least. Free-kicks and, occasionally, penalties have bumped up his already immense contribution to the side – he finished as United's top FA Cup scorer in 1995, with four.

Irwin's ability to operate on either flank has been tested at the highest level – Jack Charlton rewarding the work-rate and consistency of the slight defender with two caps during USA '94.

Against the Netherlands in the second round, the Irish dream was to evaporate in the Florida heat – without Denis in the team.

DENIS IRWIN
Defender

Birthplace:	Cork
D.O.B:	31st October 1965
Height:	5'8"
Transferred from:	Oldham Athletic 8.6.90
Previous Clubs:	Leeds United, Oldham
United Debut:	25.8.90 vs Coventry City
Full International	Republic of Ireland

DENIS IRWIN
LEAGUE RECORD FOR UNITED

Season	Apps	Goals
1990-91	33(1)	0
1991-92	37(1)	4
1992-93	40	5
1993-94	42	2
1994-95	40	2
Total	192(2)	13

DENIS IRWIN
INTERNATIONAL FOR REPUBLIC OF IRELAND

Debut:	12.1.90 vs Morocco
Appearances	36
Goals	1

SHARP

Steve Bruce

It had to happen – the symbolic rock on which United's prolific nineties success was built reached 'a certain age'. Though defenders have continued past their mid-thirties before (John Wark was still turning out for Ipswich in the top flight at 37 last season), the pace of the game is increasing to the extent where a tactical dip into a lower division in some new role might make sense. So thought Derby County. United said: 'Ohh no, – Brucie is here to stay'.

STEVE'S UTTER REFUSAL TO THROW IN THE TOWEL ENSURES HIS PLACE IN THE OLD TRAFFORD HALL OF FAME

A one-time team-mate of Peter Beardsley back home in Wallsend, Steve has always been the rugged one in a team of pretty boys!

When he joined club captain Bryan Robson on the steps of the main stand at Old Trafford to collect the first Premiership in 1993, his face said it all. The bogey was laid, and the work ethic he epitomises had been every bit as responsible as the fancy stuff.

One player truly entitled to scratch his head at the centre-halves who have found themselves ahead of him in the queue for England caps, Brucie never let bitterness cloud his commitment to the England B side – and what is more, Bobby Robson took the time last year to confide how he now felt that he'd made a big mistake in overlooking him.

Signed from Norwich in 1987, goals were soon to become the unlikely trademark of the Geordie stopper. He was certainly the hero in Warsaw, when United broke the backs of Legia in the European Cup Winners' Cup semi-final first leg back in April, 1991.

However, it was Steve's utter refusal to throw in the towel when defeat stared the Reds in the face at home to Sheffield Wednesday in the 1993 run-in that ensures his place in the Old Trafford hall of fame.

As time was extended to an excruciating nine minutes and the memory of '92's late championship blow-up at home to Nottingham Forest threatened to recur, up stepped Steve with two unstoppable headers to send Kiddo and the Boss into a display of unrestrained euphoria on the pitch in full view of *Match of the Day*'s watching millions!

Despite suffering at the hands of zealous officials and their interpretation both of the offside and tackle-from-behind laws, Steve was rewarded with a new contract last season, having postponed a hernia operation in a desperate bid to keep the Reds on the glory trail.

He can always go into film-making when his latest deal expires, as the man behind the intimate work *Captain's Log* and its sequel.

STEVE BRUCE
Defender

Birthplace:	Newcastle-upon-Tyne
D.O.B:	31st December 1960
Height:	6'0"
Transferered from:	Norwich City 31.12.87
Previous Clubs:	Gillingham, Norwhich City
United Debut:	19.12.87 vs Portsmouth

STEVE BRUCE
LEAGUE RECORD FOR UNITED

Season	Apps	Goals
1987-88	21	2
1988-89	38	2
1989-90	34	3
1990-91	31	13
1991-92	37	5
1992-93	42	5
1993-94	41	3
1994-95	35	2
Total	279	35

BRUCE
4
UMBRO

Gary Pallister

Despite a complete absence of good fortune, 1994/'95 was arguably Gary's best in a United shirt. Particularly for his handling of Alan Shearer; a formidable blend of composure; 'getting a foot in' and improved use of the ball, he deserved more praise. With an appearance in the abandoned Dublin game, Pally's England season was forgettable when not marred by injury – the luck even rubbed off when Collymore wore the number six shirt on his blank debut!

HE POSSESSES A PHYSICAL PRESENCE AND COMFORT ON THE BALL THE ENVY OF THE PREMIERSHIP, WITH THE CAPS TO PROVE IT

Daisy or Dolly? Dolly Daydream is the nickname the Boss plumped for to describe the 'laid-back' half of the Pally/Bruce combo, one which, when split up, means United's hopes of playing their normal running game are invariably adversely affected.

One reason for separation last season was the skipper's unfortunate appetite for suspension – whilst England regular Gary managed to avoid even a yellow card until April!

He even played a part, unlike the majority of the first team, in the club's brief Coca-Cola Cup campaign, partnering Keane, May and Bruce in the process.

Though now seen as potentially the best central defender in Europe by his manager – having mastered the 'grip' that makes a great centre-half – his arrival from Middlesbrough in September 1989 at £2.3m was hardly greeted with unanimous approval.

A rainy midweek home debut saw Norwich win with a penalty conceded by a nervous Pallister, and three weeks later came the 5-1 crash at Maine Road.

Gary set about building himself up physically (mental toughness was always going to come with the territory at the heart of the defence – United's longstanding problem area), and his confidence soon blossomed.

The former docks wages clerk and Northern League 2nd Division beanpole now possesses a physical presence and comfort on the ball the envy of the Premiership, with the caps to prove it.

Despite the nightmare in Barcelona, Pally never had a more consistently outstanding season - including '92 and his PFA Player of the Year award.

His nodded goal against Crystal Palace from a Neville throw-in was, in its way, just as vital as the Hughes volley which also kept the Double dream alive at the identical FA Cup semi-final stage twelve months earlier.

GARY PALLISTER
Defender

Birthplace:	Ramsgate
D.O.B:	30th June 1965
Height:	6'4"
Transferred from:	Middlesbrough 28.8.89
Previous Clubs:	Mboro, Darlington (loan)
United Debut:	30.8.89 vs Norwich City
Full International	England

GARY PALLISTER
LEAGUE RECORD FOR UNITED

Season	Apps	Goals
1989-90	35	3
1990-91	36	0
1991-92	37(3)	1
1992-93	42	1
1993-94	41	1
1994-95	42	2
Total	233(3)	8

GARY PALLISTER
INTERNATIONAL FOR ENGLAND

Debut:	27.4.88 vs Hungary
Appearances	18
Goals	0

MENTAL TOUGHNESS WAS ALWAYS GOING TO COME WITH THE TERRITORY AT THE HEART OF THE DEFENCE – UNITED'S LONGSTANDING PROBLEM AREA

David May

David grew up, in football terms, in the quiet backwater of Blackburn before the injection of Jack Walker's millions. Able to develop at his own pace, he took to Premiership football with ease at the age of 22. He made his debut against Rovers at Wembley in the 1994 Charity Shield but soon found the demands of full-back alien to his natural centre-half role. Dave is now hungry for the chance to spoil his old mates' party after their first title in 81 years.

WHAT HELPED DAVID FEEL MOST AT HOME WAS HIS THIRD GOAL OF '94/'95 – THE WINNER AGAINST SHEFFIELD WEDNESDAY AS THE TITLE RACE REALLY HOTTED UP

The problem with David May is... he's a Blue! He certainly must have regretted letting that little nugget slip so soon after United's £1m+ swoop for the out-of-contract Blackburn defensive star. Players usually manage to keep such information quiet - and play on the 'local boy made good' angle instead.

Showing an admirable sense of humour if nothing else, the Oldham-born six-footer entered his side in the 1994 Manchester United Staff Fantasy League and called it MCFC.

David played in more games than anyone could have foreseen before injury struck down stalwart right-back Paul Parker. It has to be said that it took Parker three years to work out a partnership with Andrei Kanchelskis, a player not noted as a tackling machine. May was expected in some quarters to reproduce this understanding overnight.

On the left, Denis Irwin so rarely gets over-run because both Giggsy and Sharpe are able to look after business themselves along 'I'll scratch your back, you scratch mine' lines. David had no such luxury, and. alongside unfamiliar team-mates. was forced to adapt to a position, an offside trap and a style of play that was entirely new to him.

Once drafted in to Steve Bruce's role, however, the contrast in his confidence and proficiency was there for all to see. May and Pallister were magnificent in tandem at Highbury, then his valuable header that secured a point against Crystal Palace at Selhurst Park in January was destined to be overlooked, for obvious reasons.

Still, what helped David feel most at home was his third goal of last term – the winner against Sheffield Wednesday as the title pace really hotted up. It took him only five minutes to get on the end of a corner and settle the nerves of the whole sell-out crowd. Sadly, once again a total absence of fortune saw him limp out of the rest of the season 20 minutes later with a pulled back muscle he had sustained in the warm-up!

No FA Cup Final for David then – but no doubt there was some doubting Thomas in the stands who found a way of blaming him for Paul Rideout's sucker-punch header that won the game with the Reds caught upfield.

DAVID MAY
Defender

Birthplace:	Oldham
D.O.B:	24th June 1970
Height:	6'0"
Transferred from:	Blackburn Rovers 1.7.94
Previous Clubs:	Blackburn Rovers
United Debut:	20.8.94 vs Q.P.R

DAVID MAY
LEAGUE RECORD FOR UNITED

Season	Apps	Goals
1994-95	15(4)	2
Total	15(4)	2

HIS VALUABLE HEADER THAT SECURED A POINT AGAINST CRYSTAL PALACE AT SEL-HURST PARK IN JANUARY WAS DESTINED TO BE OVERLOOKED

United Europe

When it comes to comprehending the standing of Manchester United in the history of the game, a bald list of dates and places could never suffice. Wherever you may wander, you'll find some enthusiast with a dodgy pronunciation of Nobby Stiles. Why? Chiefly because, in leading English clubs out of the isolationist straitjacket insisted upon by our football authorities (Hibs played in the *very* first European Cup), United blazed a trail so cruelly halted over Munich. That's why.

29-5-68, WEMBLEY STADIUM
STEPNEY
BRENNAN
DUNNE
CRERAND
FOULKES
STILES
BEST
KIDD
CHARLTON
SADLER
ASTON

15-5-91, FEYENOORD STADIUM, ROTTERDAM
SEALEY
IRWIN
BLACKMORE
BRUCE
PALLISTER
ROBSON
INCE
PHELAN
McCLAIR
HUGHES
SHARPE

It was the United of Matt Busby, under one-time England player, chairman Harold Hardman, that defied the edicts of the FA back in 1956/57 to take the club into the second edition of the Champions' Cup – giving a lead for other English teams to follow.

Despite the incalculable human tragedy of the Munich air crash during the club's second assault on the competition (the semi-final had been reached at the first time of asking), Busby's vision ensured that the name of Manchester United would come to be celebrated on a truly worldwide scale.

Ever since those early expeditions (and participation in the annual Zurich Youth tournament, dating from '53 to the present day), the unique prestige of Continental competition and Busby's determination to make footballing friends far beyond the Manchester skyline have combined to generate floodlit nights of rare and compulsive exhilaration – encapsulated in the capture of the European Cup itself at Wembley in 1968, against Benfica of Portugal.

So much blood sweat and tears had been invested in the pursuit of the Cup that television coverage brought the whole nation together – just two years after the World Cup had been secured at the same stadium by an England side containing United greats Bobby Charlton and Nobby Stiles. Denis Law may have been forced to observe – injured – from a hospital bed, but that night George Best, Paddy Crerand, Alex Stepney and fresh-faced birthday boy Brian Kidd were not found wanting, as extra time could only delay a historic 4-1 triumph.

As the first English club team to win the highest honour in the game, United's legend was assured. Since '68, successive managers have striven to see MUFC go into the hat by satisfying that awesome criteria for qualification – the status of champions. Before he won the Premiership, however, Alex Ferguson delighted the fans and stirred many a distant memory with his victory in the Cup Winners' Cup of 1991.

By winning in Montpellier, Warsaw and 2-1 in the Rotterdam final against newly-crowned Spanish League winners Barcelona, United once again took a skilful and gutsy brand of football and showed what they were made of on a dazzling, wet night that saw Mark Hughes steal the show against his former club.

United topped off that year by securing the Super Cup – contested between Champions' Cup and Cup Winners' Cup holders – with a McClair goal in a single leg encounter with Red Star Belgrade at Old Trafford.

The European scene demands that Manchester United play a part – and even as the club set out to win the UEFA Cup for the very first time, aficionados far beyond these shores will be stealing themselves for that day when the Reds renew their quest for the club's undisputed holy grail... the European Champions' Cup itself.

The Youths

More than any other club's in the country, Manchester United's youth policy is renowned for spotting talent and developing it, from the Busby Babes of yesteryear to Fergie's Fledglings of the nineties – the current proud holders of the FA Youth Cup.

Hand in hand with a European pedigree established in the fifties goes the tradition of the very best players nurtured, from school days, within the fold of the club – a tradition made famous by the Busby Babes.

United won the League Championship in 1956 and '57 with a team of such tender age they threatened to dominate the domestic game for years to come – a supremacy interrupted by the death of eight players on a German airstrip in February, 1958.

Of them, Duncan Edwards, David Pegg, Geoff Bent, Roger Byrne, Mark Jones and Eddie Colman – besides survivors Jackie Blanchflower, Johnny Berry (neither of whom played again); Bobby Charlton and Wilf McGuinness – were all groomed in Manchester – wherever they came from in the first place.

Now, founded on a series of 'centres of excellence' around Britain and Ireland, the Babes tradition has been revived by Alex Ferguson. It was a priority from his first days in charge to address the scouting system, and, though Busby's record of five successive FA Youth Cups ('53-'57) will take some beating, coach Eric Harrison has put the trophy in the cabinet twice, in 1992 and '95, and what is more, has supplied the first team with the likes of the following: Walsh, the Nevilles, Robins, Beckham, O'Kane, Scholes, Butt, Thornley and of course, Giggs.

Norman Whiteside, christened the Shankill Skinhead on turning up at 15 with his boots in a plastic bag, pre-dated Harrison's arrival, but helped United to a Lancs Youth Cup win at Maine Road in 1981 in the company of future seniors Clayton Blackmore, Billy Garton and a certain Mark Hughes.

Now, waiting in the wings are the likes of Terry Cooke, whose penalty won the '95 final shoot-out against Tottenham; Jovan Kirovski, who has already played a dozen games for the USA, Chris Casper, an England Youth and under 21 cap now vying with Pat McGibbon for a senior slot, and John Curtis, last season's England schoolboys captain.

'Home-grown' was the policy that underlay the Busby dynasty – and the youth set-up presided over by the current regime has ensured the future is in equally safe hands.

(LEFT) ENGLAND SCHOOLBOY CAPTAIN DUNCAN EDWARDS GREETS HIS SCOTTISH COUNTERPART

TODAY'S CROP INCLUDES (L-R): KIROVSKI, COOKE (WITH CUP), CASPER AND O'KANE

Nicky Butt

Hard-as-nails Nicky was widely acknowledged to be United's best performer on a disastrous night in Barcelona in November 1994. He refused to let the clinical finishing of Romario and Stoitchkov detract from his mission to pull United pack into the match. That was just the taste of things to come, as he went on to grab the FA Cup semi-final by the scruff of the neck when given the second half in place of Beckham. At last the word is out – Butt's about!

HIS EXPERIENCE WAS ALSO GREATLY ENHANCED WITH THE VISIT TO AUSTRALIA FOR THE 1993 JUNIOR WORLD CUP

Having been used to good effect in the Euro campaign of '93/'94, Butt was no stranger to supporters by the following season – but his incredible progress still made everyone sit up and take notice.

Gorton lad Nicky may have a Scottish dad, but his international prospects are firmly wrapped up in the England camp.

He has worn an England shirt at every level up to under 21, where he has been essential to the side that has all but qualified for the junior version of the 1996 European Championships.

His experience was also greatly enhanced with the visit to Australia for the 1993 Junior World Cup, in which England came third after losing in the semi-finals to Ghana.

He has an FA Youth Cup medal from 1992 to offset the disappointment of losers' medals from the '93 Youth Cup and this year's Wembley defeat at the hands of Everton. Following the first semi-final at Villa Park, which ended 2-2 back in April, Alex Ferguson confessed at the press conference: "Butt has now reached the point where I can't leave him out."

Nicky's tough-tackling midfield exploits have given the Boss the confidence to let the mantle of Paul Ince fall on the 20-year-old's shoulders in the wake of the one-time England skipper's multi-million pound deal with Internazionale. Confidence that may have surprised many outside the club – but not inside.

The Buttster scored a beauty of a first Premiership goal on the South Coast on New Year's Eve against Southampton, but last season also saw Nicky fall victim to a flurry of unusual problems that kept him out of the side – starting at Villa Park in November, when he lost a couple of teeth in a clash with former under 21 colleague Ugo Ehiogu.

NICKY BUTT
Midfield

Birthplace:	Manchester
D.O.B:	21st January 1975
Height:	5'10"
Signed trainee:	8.7.91
Signed professional:	23.1.93
United Debut:	21.11.92 vs Oldham

NICKY BUTT
LEAGUE RECORD FOR UNITED

Season	Apps	Goals
1992-93	0(1)	0
1993-94	0(1)	0
1994-95	11(11)	1
Total	11(13)	1

Unfortunately, double vision was another source of concern, along with flu and a full complement of more conventional knocks.

Before Bryan Robson left to take up the job of player-manager at Ayresome Park, he nominated the one player who stood out from all the other promising youngsters at the club's disposal – it was bound to be a midfielder... and it was Butt.

SHARP

Roy Keane

April proved a cruel month for Roy Keane: full-back Sunday 2nd; centre-half at Villa Park on the 9th; then into midfield for the FA Cup semi-final replay, in which he sustained a first-half ankle wound needing seven stitches, before steaming, despite the Boss wanting him off, straight out into a second-half encounter with Gareth Southgate to earn the first red card of his career. All this, the apology, a subdued final and surgery behind him, Roy just can't wait...

HIS VERSATILITY WAS NEVER MORE IN EVIDENCE THAN DURING UNITED'S BID FOR A DOUBLE DOUBLE LAST TERM

There was no outcry along the lines of 'dizzy transfer spiral' when Keano enlisted with the Reds in June, 1993 for a British record £3.75m.

Snapped up from relegated Nottingham Forest, with rivals Blackburn and Arsenal beaten to his signature, there was also the conspicuous absence of the word 'gamble', which usually accompanies any fee of such scale – not to mention that well-worn, treacherous path from the City Ground to Old Trafford besides.

What is more, the Irishman's fierce competitive instincts were enough to persuade Alex Ferguson that his alleged favourite, Brian McClair and his own son, Darren, were no longer worthy of a regular place. In his first season United claimed the Double.

Less happily, in addition to a hamstring injury picked up in November '94, a hernia operation had to be delayed from October to season's end such was his commitment to the Red cause.

Still an amateur boxer when first noticed by Brian Clough playing for Cobh Ramblers, the £10,000 spent bringing Roy to England wouldn't now buy a toe-nail!

Clough's old assistant at the City Ground, Ronnie Fenton, having finally shaken hands on what was then a record deal between British clubs, told Alex Ferguson: "You've just signed the best centre-half in the country there, " – and his versatility was never more in evidence than during United's bid for a double Double last term.

Season '94/'95 saw Keane turn out at full-back, centre-half and all over the middle, with the goal supply the only area of his game that was to suffer.

Even so, away from home, due to Keane's fabled penchant for getting from 'box to box', no one is more vital to the Reds' ability to turn defence into attack. Perhaps it was no coincidence that Ireland's first real hiccups in qualifying for Euro '96 came as Roy convalesced in July.

With Paul Ince gone, the opportunity to dominate the middle of the park that Roy has yearned for has arrived.

ROY KEANE
Midfield

Birthplace:	Cork
D.O.B:	10th August 1971
Height:	5'10"
Transferred from:	Nottingham Forest 19.7.93
Previous Clubs:	Cobh Ramblers, Forest
United Debut:	15.8.93 vs Norwich City
Full International:	Republic of Ireland

ROY KEANE
LEAGUE RECORD FOR UNITED

Season	Apps	Goals
1993-94	34(3)	5
1994-95	23(2)	2
Total	57(5)	7

ROY KEANE
INTERNATIONAL FOR REPUBLIC OF IRELAND

Debut:	26.5.91 vs Chile
Appearances	28
Goals	1

WITH PAUL INCE GONE, THE OPPORTUNITY TO DOMINATE THE MIDDLE OF THE PARK THAT ROY HAS YEARNED FOR HAS ARRIVED

David Beckham

The history of London lads taken into the United fold is a long one, with Alex Stepney, the sixties goalkeeper, the longest serving, at twelve years. David also has the cult status achieved by Gordon Hill, Ray Wilkins, Les Sealey and Paul Ince to comfort him should he ever feel alienated from the crowd. The difference is that Beckham plumped for the Reds from school rather than costing the club big money. Can he make the chant 'king of all cockneys' his own?

DAVID STEPPED UP TO THE PLATE AGAINST GALATASARAY AT HOME WITH HIGH EXPECTATIONS TO LIVE UP TO

Tied down to a four-year contract after a run to the semi-finals of the annual summer Toulon under 21 tournament in France with England, this London-born schemer is all set for a bright future at Old Trafford.

The son of United-mad parents who follow him to every game, his impact was most spectacular last season in the final game of United's ill-fated Champions' League campaign, back in December, 1994.

Having impressed with his appetite for and intelligent use of the ball in Coca-Cola Cup ties against Port Vale and Newcastle, David stepped up to the plate against Galatasaray at home with high expectations to live up to.

Bryan Robson was not alone when he picked Beckham out as one of the best passers at the club – but it was to be his marksmanship that would be stealing the headlines on this occasion. He struck, from outside the area, an arrow of a shot into the far corner past a stunned Gintaras Stauce, the Turk side's handy Polish goalkeeper, to make the score 2-0 on a night when running out 4-0 winners still saw the Reds crash out.

The Eastender's very first senior appearance came as substitute for Andrei Kanchelskis in a Coca-Cola Cup 3rd round tie at Brighton in 1992, a game drawn thanks to a stunning Danny Wallace volley.

In both '95 FA Cup quarter and semi-finals, Beckham was handed a wide role in the absence of the sidelined Ukrainian winger, with a Premiership outing at home to Leeds sandwiched in between.

Though his coolness on the ball did not desert him, he was a fish out of water when plucked from the middle, and when Nicky Butt replaced him at Villa Park against Palace, the balance of the match changed as McClair was the man chosen to shift out wide.

David gained valuable experience at Preston North End in '94, when his lone spell included one goal straight from a corner!

Far from having been put in the 'shop window', however, as many loan deals are designed to achieve, this welcome spell of truly competitive first-team football was another vital step in Beckham's route to the top.

DAVID BECKHAM
MIDFIELD

Birthplace:	Leytonstone
D.O.B:	2nd May 1975
Height:	6'0"
Signed trainee:	8.7.91
Signed Professional:	23.1.93
United Debut:	2.4.95 vs Leeds United

DAVID BECKHAM
LEAGUE RECORD FOR UNITED

Season	Apps	Goals
1994-95	2(2)	0
Total	2(2)	0

IN BOTH '95 FA CUP QUARTER AND SEMI-FINALS, BECKHAM WAS HANDED A WIDE ROLE IN THE ABSENCE OF THE SIDELINED KANCHELSKIS

Brian McClair

The man they called 'teacher' when he guided a team of fledglings through the Coca-Cola Cup ties against Port Vale in 1994 could have been playing for Aston Villa had he not heeded the call of higher education – and home-sickness – by quitting the Midlands in his teens. Of such lasting value to the squad because of his tireless desire for the ball, 'Choccy' said goodbye to mass adulation with his move from forward to a deeper role prior to the arrival of Cantona.

HIS EXPERIENCE AND ABILITY TO IMPART THE MANAGER'S TACTICAL AND MOTIVATIONAL KNOW-HOW OUT ON THE PITCH HAS BEEN INVALUABLE

The departure of Gary Walsh will left Choccy as the club's longest-serving player, having arrived from Celtic back in 1987 in a tribunal-assessed deal that still has then-boss Billy McNeill fuming at his old playing adversary Alex Ferguson!

For £850,000 United had found a born-winner; non-stop worker and thinker about the game – who was to beat Gordon Hill's twelve year-old goal tally of 22 with 31 in his first season – also making him the first player to score over 2o league goal in a season since George Best.

Amongst the many, many games dominated by this Mathematics graduate, one derby fixture, at Maine Road back in 1991, with the Reds seemingly dead and buried at 3-1 down, particularly stands out. McClair took matters in hand and administered two late goals to leave the Blues reeling and in sudden dread of losing!

Afterwards he was to say: "I think we are now seeing more and more players accepting the challenge and responsibility that goes with playing for Manchester United."

Though his contribution seems destined to be forever unsung, Choccy's talents are not lost on his colleagues – apart from the amount of ball they trust him with, they also trust him with the players' pool and he is seen, along with his pal Pat Nevin, as an important future figure in the administration of the game.

Whereas many players fear the jack-of-all-trades tag, McClair's reaction to a Schmeichel injury last December was to tell the boss: "Hey, I haven't played in goal yet..."

His experience and ability to impart the manager's tactical and motivational know-how out on the pitch has been invaluable since the departure of Bryan Robson.

BRIAN McCLAIR

Forward

Birthplace:	Airdrie
D.O.B:	8th December 1963
Height:	5'10"
Transferred from:	Celtic 1.7.87
Previous Clubs:	Villa, Motherwell, Celtic
United Debut:	15.8.87 vs Southampton
Full International	Scotland

BRIAN McCLAIR

LEAGUE RECORD FOR UNITED

Season	Apps	Goals
1987-88	40	24
1988-89	38	10
1989-90	37	5
1990-91	34(2)	13
1991-92	41(1)	18
1992-93	41(1)	9
1993-94	12(14)	1
1994-95	35(5)	5
Total	278(23)	85

BRIAN McCLAIR

INTERNATIONAL FOR SCOTLAND

Debut:	2.12.87 vs Luxembourg
Appearances	30
Goals	2

UMBRO
SHARP
Mitre

Silverware

Fergie's haul: two Premierships, two FA Cups, a League Cup, Super Cup, two FA Youth Cups and a European Cup Winners' Cup – including the Double and sundry individual awards. Ron Atkinson won two FA Cups, the Doc one (and promotion). Sir Matt was responsible for five championships, two FA Cups, three Charity Shields, six FA Youth Cups and the European Champions' Cup, whilst Ernest Magnall brings up the rear with two championships and an FA Cup.

THE LAW MAN ROUNDS GORDON BANKS IN THE LEICESTER GOAL TO SCORE THE FIRST IN UNITED'S 3-1 WEMBLEY WIN IN 1963

Manchester United's forebears, Newton Heath, formed in 1878, were not blessed with the honours that would in time turn the Old Trafford club into a candidate for the biggest in the world.

The most success seen by the team in yellow and green was runners-up spot in the 2nd Division of 1896/'7 to Notts County, and, in an inauspicious FA Cup Preliminary Round debut, in 1886, Fleetwood Rangers took the tie by default when Heath's players refused to play extra time.

Manchester United, as Newton Heath became in 1902, went on to claim the FA Cup a joint record eight times, and the Championship (if you include the break-away FA Premiership) nine. Ernest Magnall presided over title wins in 1908 and '11 and the FA Cup in 1909: the days of Billy Meredith. Still, the summit of the Red Devils' domestic achievements undoubtedly came in 1994, with the claiming of the Double – a feat only matched by Preston, Aston Villa, Spurs, Arsenal and Liverpool.

Although a formidable international reputation had already been forged before the 1960s, it was this decade that saw United stake their claim in terms of historical supremacy over the latter two clubs. As much of an admirer of Busby as Bill Shankly was, the ethic he installed at Anfield bore more fruit, with four European Cup wins after his departure and a formidable '80s stranglehold on the title under Bob Paisley. Similarly, those who depict Highbury as the "home of football" point to the feats of Herbert Chapman in the '30s, when United were, relatively speaking, slumming it between the divisions before the recruitment of a de-mobbed Busby in 1945.

Former City and Liverpool player Busby set about assembling the first of his three celebrated United sides – the first trophy being hoisted by converted full-back Johnny Carey at Wembley after a thrilling FA Cup Final defeat of Blackpool in 1948. A trial of patience followed, as the 1st Division was not clinched until 1952 – following four second places in five seasons. This team, containing names such as Jack Rowley, Crompton and Pearson, was to be dismantled without sentiment as Busby sought to bring in the Babes that had so gripped the public's imagination – led by the immaculate Byrne, Edwards and Colman, but augmented by key signings like Taylor, Wood and the ex-miner, Foulkes.

Bobby Charlton had the good fortune to break into a side with the football world at its feet; two consecutive titles – the first in '56 – with a Double foiled by Aston Villa at Wembley in '57, saw to it that if he played, more often than not it was out of position!

Munich, needless to say, meant that a heap of responsibility was thrust onto his shoulders – something he was never to shirk throughout his distinguished career.

TOP LEFT: FERGIE AND KIDDO SHOW OFF '94'S BOUNTY
RIGHT: NORMAN WHITESIDE WITH THE 1985 FA CUP WON WITH HIS LEFT BOOT
BOTTOM: PAUL INCE PARADES THE FA CUP AFTER 1990'S REPLAYED FINAL

Meanwhile, the Boss was persuaded to pick up the reins once more and build yet another team to meet the challenge of United's destiny.

Relying on hindsight, with Denis Law added to a new, solid crop comprising fellow Scot Crerand; Stiles, Dunne and the mercurial George Best, the cliché 'last piece in the jigsaw' is irresistible. The Aberdonian's finishing power is not always fully recognised when his profile is compared with that of those team-mates who would share his distinction of being voted European Footballer of The Year: Best and Charlton.

Still, whatever the billing, this Englishman, Irishman and Scotsman routine wiped the smile off most of the biggest names in the game in their all-too-brief reign. Champions in '65 and '7 (though Best would miss 1963's FA Cup, win as would Law the Champions' Cup in '68), perhaps more important than the stats was the fact that at times, United laid on some of the most glorious football England has ever seen.

Wilf McGuinness stepped from dressing room to hot-seat, and found some only too happy to exploit his lack of seniority when he replaced the newly-knighted Busby in 1969. Two semi-finals in his first season was not deemed satisfactory, and a barren spell ensued, during which the team broke up and was taken down by Tommy Docherty.

The Doc bounced back and won the FA Cup in 1977, simultaneously preventing a Liverpool Double, but, as had been the case when the interim appointment, Frank O'Farrell's good sense and dignity was sacrificed on the altar of charisma, Dave Sexton – the Doc's own successor – was to pay the price for not replenishing the trophy cabinet. He was fired in May 1991.

Ron Atkinson was to sign Bryan Robson, an all-time United great, and in '83 and '5 took him to two of his record three FA Cup wins as captain – the last coming via Ferguson in 1990. But Big Ron's fragile sides were not cut out for the big one, and he gave way to Fergie, the scourge of Glasgow's Old Firm, in 1986. He has gone on to win seven senior cups in the last five years.

Of the less coveted competitions, United's record in the League (currently Coca-Cola) Cup was abysmal until the '90s, and the trophy represented scant consolation for 1992's Premier League suicide. United have claimed the Charity Shield thrice, sharing it four times, whilst ventures into the Watney ('69/'70); Anglo-Italian (late '60s), and an early version of the Screensport Super Cup (mid-'80s) respectively put nothing new on the sideboard.

With the amount of games in a season now long past the oppressive stage, priority in the future will inevitably be placed on the Championship and FA Cup sponsored by Littlewoods. Valuable experience was gained in the first team in 1994 by the likes of Scholes, O'Kane, Casper, Beckham and Tomlinson; there was certainly no disgrace in bowing out to Newcastle in the CCC third round on their own patch, having pluckily dispatched Port Vale. Even after the seniors' traumatic, empty-handed finale, the Boss had no qualms about having effectively jettisoned what is now a competition of less and less relevance to the game's top clubs.

Andy Cole

***The Voice* newspaper may have splashed 'WORTH EVERY PENNY' over its January 17 back page, but the consensus marked Andy Cole down for a foolish waste of plc cash and, as the right wing slot fell vacant on the eve of 1995/'96, the loss of Keith Gillespie to rivals Newcastle in the exchange was also judged to have been a major blunder. The quicksilver goal-getter himself remains defiant. His claim is simple: he's done it everywhere else, so why not here?**

COLE'S GOAL RATIO DOES NOT GUARANTEE FIVE EVERY GAME, BUT IT DOES ILLUSTRATE WHAT SHEER PACE AND INSTINCT CAN DO TO ANY DEFENCE

The rumour-mongering was into overdrive by the time Andy made his debut for United back in January following his out-of-the-blue £6m move from Kevin Keegan's Toon Army. Had there been a bust-up? What vile habits were behind the sudden offloading of the prolific marksman? Cole just got on with it.

The goal-less minutes were scrupulously logged; Cantona, Scholes, McClair, Hughes, Giggs (and even, briefly, Steve Bruce!) all enjoyed the pace, intelligence and work-rate of the newcomer upfront... and the goals came.

Pure opportunism – a virtue so often neglected in favour of style by the Reds over the years – was at work for the first, against Villa; then a deftness and speed of reaction a week later against City.

The end of the world was the general verdict of the experts after defeat at Goodison Park, but April 4 saw the record book sail merrily out of the window to the sound of a thousand eaten words as Ipswich were dismantled and Andy went from two goals in six to seven out of seven with the soon-to-be-relegated Ipswich Town demolished 9-0 at Old Trafford.

Style-wise, a post-Hughes United will never be the same again. The Old Trafford goal tap – which the Welshman always threatened, but never quite managed to increase from a drip – could yet turn out to be a hydrant.

He may not be the first to arrive boasting the midas touch, and Cole's career ratio – which stands comparison with the world's best – does not guarantee five every game, but it does illustrate what sheer pace and instinct can do to any defence, however packed.

With the stark emptiness following Upton Park, Andy's last-gasp misses, and whether he can work with Shearer in an England shirt raised questions in the mind of many a loyal Red. Once over his shin splints problem, the answers are there all right – tucked inside Cole's size 8½ boots.

ANDY COLE
Forward

Birthplace:	Nottingham
D.O.B:	15th October 1971
Height:	5'11"
Transferred from:	Newcastle United 12.1.95
Previous Clubs:	Arsenal, Newcastle United, Bristol City, Fulham(loan)
United Debut:	22.1.95 vs Blackburn
Full International	England

ANDY COLE
LEAGUE RECORD FOR UNITED

Season	Apps	Goals
1994-95	17(1)	12
Total	17(1)	12

ANDY COLE
INTERNATIONAL FOR ENGLAND

Debut:	29.3.94 vs Uruguay
Appearances	1 as sub
Goals	0

Paul Scholes

There is something about a homegrown talent with an eye for goal which fires the imagination of any club's supporters – and Manchester United's demanding fans are no exception. With the deceptive appearance of a welterweight boxer, the last thing they expected of him was a delicate touch and appreciation of positional play that has been every bit as impressive as the goal per game he delivered in his breakthrough season.

THERE WAS A CLEVER, LATE LOB IN THE 2-2 DRAW WITH BARCELONA THAT CAME SO CLOSE TO STEALING THE SHOW

Never a player to inspire awe in the uninitiated spectator or opposing defence, this Salford-born pocket playmaker and goal-poacher came of age in his selective exposure to first-team football during the 1994/'95 campaign.

With a goal ratio to match the best, Paul transferred the form which helped United to the Reserves' title in '93/'4 into the Premiership – with a variety of partners – and could easily have been the man to secure the first double Double in British football history, had Neville Southall and Ludek Miklosko not turned on the heroics and beaten out his efforts against Everton and West Ham United in May.

Having got off the mark on his full debut at Vale Park in September with two expertly taken goals, Scholesy ended up at Highfield Road in May scoring United's first in the classic five-goal encounter with Coventry and looking every inch the senior.

In between there was a clever, late lob in the 2-2 draw with Barcelona that came so close to stealing the show; a piece of the action in the Camp Nou, and opportunistic strikes against Ipswich and QPR away, then Coventry at home. Two fine exhibitions of prompting work from deep at Manchester City and at home to Sheffield Wednesday revealed his maturity and versatility.

Comparisons have abounded – from a young Dalglish to Eric the King himself – but the comparisons that will matter career-wise are with the likes of Andy Ritchie and Mark Robins – homegrown natural scorers who, after an initial impact, left United, unable to break out of the shadow of the big money strikers available. Supporters look back on their contributions all the more fondly for their having been locally-born, but there are no prizes for your birth certificate when the day comes for the manager to assess his most potent permutations in the hardest position of all.

Scholes' link play suggests that the ginger schemer has the talent to lay such fears to rest. There is also time for MUFC's Young Player of the Year 1993 to join clubmates David Beckham, Nicky Butt and Chris Casper in making headway at under 21 level with England in the season to come.

PAUL SCHOLES
Forward

Birthplace:	Salford
D.O.B:	16th November 1974
Height:	5'7"
Signed trainee:	8.7.91
Signed professional:	23.1.93.
United Debut:	24.9.93 vs Ipswich Town

PAUL SCHOLES
LEAGUE RECORD FOR UNITED

Season	Apps	Goals
1994-95	6(11)	5
Total	6(11)	5

COMPARISONS HAVE ABOUNDED – FROM A YOUNG DALGLISH TO ERIC THE KING HIMSELF

Lee Sharpe

After the succession of inventive hairstyles sported by Lee since his arrival in 1988 – including one memorable, permed centre-parting – no one should have been surprised when he waltzed into training with a skinhead before 1995/'96 got under way. The Lee Sharpe Fan Club – numbering over 2,500 (and only 80 per cent males) – is not alone in hoping this season sees his electric pace and crafty crossing take him back into the England reckoning.

FIXED INDELIBLY IN MOST REDS' MINDS IS THE SPECTACULAR HAT-TRICK SCORED BY LEE AT HIGHBURY IN 1991

In sustaining a hairline fracture of the shin a matter of days after his personal highlight of '94/'95, the bubbly Brummie cast a long shadow over a campaign that had hitherto promised a route back to the international stage he first graced at the age of 19.

The left-wing wonder was pressed into service by United in midfield and at left-back – far from his own ideal position – and he performed admirably in both. The eventual decision over who fills the wide berth, however, seems no clearer between himself and soulmate Giggsy.

The visit of Barcelona to Old Trafford in October saw Lee at the top of his form and crowning a rousing, rapier display with a flicked equaliser from a blazing Ince raid that took an action replay to believe. A week later, pitched in at St James Park, he was a crock – again.

Capped by Graham Taylor before and after a bout of viral meningitis which took a serious turn for the worse back in 1992, Lee was last involved as part of the side knocked out of the World Cup in '94 by the Netherlands in Rotterdam.

Terry Venables has been happy to go along with Barnes or McManaman in tandem with Spurs' Darren Anderton since. Still, Lee holds the record for the youngest player at under 21 level, having debuted in Greece in '89 at the age of 17.

Sharpie knows how to celebrate, and his series of shuffles – the first, at Goodison Park in 1991 subsequently banned by the Boss – has included tributes both to Elvis Presley and the film *The Three Caballeros* immediately after scoring.

Fixed indelibly in most Reds' minds, however, is the spectacular hat-trick scored by Lee at Highbury in a 6-2 1991 Rumbelows Cup tie. After all, 'we want seven', with Seaman in goal, does have this ring about it...

LEE SHARPE
Forward

Birthplace:	Halesowen
D.O.B:	27th May 1971
Height:	6'0"
Transferred from:	Torquay United 1.6.88
Previous Clubs:	Torquay United
United Debut:	24.9.88 vs West Ham
Full International	England

LEE SHARPE
LEAGUE RECORD FOR UNITED

Season	Apps	Goals
1988-89	19(3)	0
1989-90	13(5)	1
1990-91	20(3)	2
1991-92	8(6)	1
1992-93	27	1
1993-94	26(4)	9
1994-95	26(2)	3
Total	139(23)	17

LEE SHARPE
INTERNATIONAL FOR ENGLAND

Debut:	27.3.91 vs Ireland
Appearances	8
Goals	0

UMBRO
SHARP
UMBRO

Eric Cantona

Banned from all football-related activity until October by the FA for his lunge at a Crystal Palace supporter, an attempt to give Cantona much-needed match-practice in July backfired in a big way. To the short-lived horror of his countless fans, he appeared to walk out on the club by jumping on a plane bound for Paris once the FA chose to question the staging of the behind-closed-doors fixture. His return after a fraught week was more than welcome.

BRYAN ROBSON WENT SO FAR AS TO SUGGEST AT ONE POINT THAT ERIC WAS ACTUALLY RUNNING THE CLUB

No one made a greater contribution to the Reds' conquest of the inaugural Premier League or historic first ever Double than the Frenchman. Fulsome were the tributes to his influence: "catalyst"; "whole new dimension"... Doyen of the playing staff Bryan Robson, who was to lose his precious number seven shirt to Eric with the introduction of squad numbers, went so far as to suggest at one point that Eric was actually running the club!

He arrived, of course, labelled 'handle with care' due to his having got through six clubs in as many years on home soil. Then he experienced decisive differences of opinion with the managers of the two English clubs to take Michel Platini's advice and gamble on his prodigious talents: Francis and Wilkinson.

The ease of his £1m signing could not have contrasted greater with the stunned reaction of pundits and public alike. His bow came as a sub in the derby – the last time he failed to score against the Blues! Only his second senior start brought his first goal, at Stamford Bridge. Apart from his goals, which have come at the rate of one in two ever since, Cantona's vision and passing – not his tackling – stand equal scrutiny. Red cards have blotted his copy book, and his outburst in January 1995 will surely never be rivalled for its shock value nor its counter-productive consequences. Whether United would have missed out on both title and FA Cup had he been around for the run-in instead of kicking his heels through a period of unprecedented press clamour will never be answered – but most observers could provide a fairly accurate verdict. Whenever and wherever he plays, however, the punters will always get their money's worth.

ERIC CANTONA
Forward

Birthplace:	Marseille, France
D.O.B:	24th May 1966
Height:	6'0"
Transferred from:	Leeds Utd 27.11.92
Previous Clubs:	Auxerre, Martigues, Olympique Marseilles, Bordeaux, Montpellier, Nimes, Leeds United
United Debut:	6.12.92 vs Man City
Full International	France

ERIC CANTONA
LEAGUE RECORD FOR UNITED

Season	Apps	Goals
1992-93	21(1)	9
1993-94	34	18
1994-95	21	12
Total	76(1)	39

ERIC CANTONA
INTERNATIONAL FOR FRANCE

Debut:	12.8.87 vs West Germany
Appearances	45
Goals	20

UMBRO
SHARP

Ryan Giggs

Without doubt one of the most gifted players ever seen at Old Trafford, Ryan's season of struggle following the Double win had all manner of theories trotted out in explanation. His girlfriend; buying a house; lucrative distractions... whilst Giggsy himself faced week after week sidelined by injury – one to his hamstring proving the most stubborn. But you've either got it or you haven't, and before long a fully-fit Ryan will have a theory of his own to trot out – on the pitch!

GIGGS CAN PERHAPS ONLY NOW CLAIM TO KNOW SOMETHING OF THE FICKLE WORLD THAT HAS BEEN AT HIS FEET SINCE HE FIRST STARTED KICKING A BALL

Few players can ever have experienced anything like the highs and lows already behind Giggsy at the age of 21. On entering last season, he could survey his having captained England schoolboys; won the FA Youth Cup; Rumbelows Cup, FA Cup, Premiership (twice) and PFA Young Player of The Year (twice). On top of this, he had broken into the Wales side at the record age of 17 and scored on full debuts for both club and country.

Though settled in his adopted Greater Manchester, details of a bid from Europe's finest, AC Milan of Italy, had reached the press and fears concerning his possible departure only added to the clamour surrounding his unassuming yet goldfish-bowl lifestyle. Following last season – initially so rich with promise – Giggs can perhaps only now claim to know something of the fickle world that has been at his feet since he first started kicking a ball. It was in September that a mere visit to the barbers made the tabloid front pages, this at a time when his failure to score in every game was beginning to irk those who viewed the steady sales of Giggs duvets with distaste and irritation. The errant studs of Edgehill in a derby that saw the less diligent Kanchelskis, on the other wing, hog the spoils with a hat-trick, had Ryan limping into the night a thoughtful, sombre figure.

Five weeks out before a difficult return to a team blowing hot and cold saw the old Giggs in all-too-rare evidence. Before the season was out, a hamstring problem would further hamper best intentions... and ultimately restricted Giggsy to a tricky 45 minutes at Wembley. The doubters will be out in force should the scintillating form that has launched so many commercial ventures once more falter. But Giggs has proved all he needs to prove – with his feet and with his attitude. One listen to a team-talk by any opposition coaching staff is ample proof of that.

RYAN GIGGS
FORWARD

Birthplace:	Cardiff
D.O.B:	29th November 1973
Height:	5'11"
Signed trainee:	9.7.90
Signed Professional:	29.11.90
United Debut:	2.3.91 vs Everton
Full International	Wales

RYAN GIGGS
LEAGUE RECORD FOR UNITED

Season	Apps	Goals
1990-91	1(1)	1
1991-92	32(6)	4
1992-93	40(1)	9
1993-94	32(6)	13
1994-95	29	1
Total	134(14)	28

RYAN GIGGS
INTERNATIONAL FOR WALES

Debut:	16.10.91 vs Germany
Appearances	13
Goals	3

SHARP

The Fans

The most numerous in the land, United supporters are an easy target for the critics, who burden them with the stigma 'glory-hunter'. For most, the jibes don't matter – they're too busy enjoying the best football around! Ferries across the Irish Sea are fit to burst for every home game – but the international attraction doesn't end there. The word has spread far and wide, putting the Reds on a par with Juventus of Italy and Barcelona of Spain in terms of widespread allegiance. "We are the pride of all Europe, the cock of the North..."

Nowhere are the supporters of a football team so renowned as the huge Red Army that follows the fortunes of Manchester United. Even when the spectacular new Old Trafford – complete with three-tier North Stand – is revealed in time for Euro'96, the projected 55,300 capacity will be unable to contain even half of the club's registered membership. Wherever the players find themselves on increasingly far-flung tours that typify the modern game, as long as they have on a United shirt, they can count on the support of a lesser or greater portion of the crowd – invariably the latter.

At a time when loss of Premiership status is associated with the spectre of financial inviability, slashed profit margins and a knock-on effect on attendances, it is stirring indeed to recall the fan crusade which swept United back into the top flight on average gates of over 50,000 back in 1975 under the inimitable stewardship of The Doc.

Similarly, how many teams would have made Wembley, as the Reds did in 1990, without a single home tie to fall back on? The invasion in turn of Nottingham, Hereford, Newcastle, Sheffield and Moss Side en route to the Twin Towers made light of United's worst league showing for many a year, and went a long way in galvanising the spirit which took the team to even greater things.

They turn up in the wind and the rain; they turn up to training; their loyalty knows no bounds. When United took on Barcelona in the 1991 ECWC Final in Rotterdam, they outnumbered the Catalans by a staggering

"THE FUTURE DEPENDS AS MUCH ON THE FERVOUR GENERATED IN THE STANDS AS ON THE PERFORMANCES OF THE SUPERSTARS..."

three to one.

As at most clubs, supporters have not always seen eye to eye with the decision-makers – from the style of football served up to the disbanding of the official Supporters Club in 1987. Issues have always been raised and debated, from Salford pub to Maltese beach – and with the advent of fanzines and lobby groups, the views of those who ultimately finance the continued growth of a club now quoted on the stock market are increasingly insistent and articulate – especially concerning seating...

One man known by now to the majority of Reds is a former postman, Burnage's Peter Boyle – aka Streaker. Having ventured onto vinyl and into print, he exemplifies the kind of supporter all too often neglected in the rush to construct the docile, Manchester-shy consumer so beloved of media stereotype. His determination to preserve the heritage of the songs sung by the terrace faithful has landed him in more than the odd scrape – but the songs live on, and whenever he is around, silence is not an option.

United remain at the top of the supporter league – they were caught only once by Liverpool in the eighties, when both clubs pulled in over one million at home for the season – with last season's grand total of 1,190,638 giving the phenomenal average attendance of 42,523.

In the first campaign restricted by the Taylor Report's demands for all-seater stadia, United's top gate came with the visit of Sheffield Wednesday – 43,868.

As the milenium approaches and facilities improve beyond recognition, the prospects for an ever-brighter future at Old Trafford depend as much on the fervour generated in the stands as on the performances of the superstars in red, white and black out on that immaculate pitch.

THE PASSION THAT SINGLES OUT UNITED SUPPORTERS IS ALIVE AND WELL IN BRYAN ROBSON (LEFT) – A PACKER IN THE MAIL ORDER DEPARTMENT AT OLD TRAFFORD, WHO FIVE YEARS AGO CHANGED HIS NAME BY DEED POLL!

Kevin Pilkington

Just as Middlesbrough were promoted into the Premiership this season, Kevin got his move upstairs when the Teeside club came in for Gary Walsh, United's erstwhile stand-in of nine years, with an offer he couldn't refuse. Having played a full part in the pre-season mini-tours of Ireland and the Far East, Kevin approached the season with these words from his specialist coach: "He's got good stability; technique; hands and presence – in fact, quite a future!"

THE MOST IMPORTANT ATTRIBUTE A GOALKEEPER CAN POSSESS IS BRAVERY, AND HE HAS THAT TO SPARE

Twenty-year-old Southerner Kevin spent a good while on the bench last term, what with injuries afflicting Schmeichel and his deputy Gary Walsh almost in turn.

With the £750,000 transfer of Gary Walsh to Bryan Robson's newly-promoted Middlesbrough side in August '95, however, Kevin's world was to suddenly become focused on that same bench like never before.

When called upon to leave the bench, his nerve was thoroughly tested, as Crystal Palace flew at the Reds in an attempt to exploit the relative inexperience of Kevin and newcomers David May and Gary Neville last November. The Premiership game, joined by Pilkington after eight minutes, was thankfully won 3-0.

Schmikes, having hurt his back in the warm-up, was unable to continue after subjecting himself to an early skirmish. After withdrawing the big Dane Alex Ferguson was to claim credit for timing the replacement just right - Irwin scored immediately from a free kick.

However, the immaculate approach Pilkington brought to bear on his big moment left a lasting impression. Former England goalkeeper Alan Hodgkinson was not surprised. Initially brought in by the Boss to look after Walsh, he has coached Kevin as well – roughly one day a week – since the lanky blond's arrival on schoolboy forms.

"I have very high hopes for Kevin. I think the most important attribute a goalkeeper can possess is bravery, and he has that to spare."

That all-too-brief Premiership experience supplemented a modest number of Pontins League games – but the big-match atmosphere will be not be lost on him, as Hodgkinson observes: "Having been one of the five substitutes for four Champions' League fixtures has given him an understanding of what it's all about at the highest level."

Replacing Walsh will be no easy task – despite his heart-rending injury record over nine years and under 50 first-team appearances, he proved a solid deputy...

"Yes, but United are so well-off for 'keepers. Paul Gibson certainly has no worries about taking Kevin's reserve place, either," was Alan's upbeat verdict.

KEVIN PILKINGTON

Goalkeeper

Birthplace:	Hitchin
D.O.B:	8th March 1974
Height:	6'2"
Signed professional:	1.7.92
United Debut:	19.11.94 vs Crystal Palace

KEVIN PILKINGTON

LEAGUE RECORD FOR UNITED

Season	Apps	GOALS
1994-95	0(1)	0
Total	0(1)	0

SHARP

Paul Parker

Was Paul Parker born too short? It's difficult to see how any player could have kept him out of his favoured central defensive role in the national team if only he could have guaranteed the aerial dominance demanded for the position. His leap is nonetheless an amazing one, yet the majority of his United career has seen him zooming up and down the right flank as the least make-shift full-back on the books. He deserves an end to his injury saga.

AS A MAN-MARKER, PAUL HAS FEW PEERS IN THE EUROPEAN GAME

Poor Paul, a familiar sight – even injured – on a matchday, with his plastercast and mobile phone. After the constant interruptions that plagued his early days at Old Trafford, he deserved better than three lousy appearances in the season that followed his first (almost) ever-present one – that of the glorious Double.

A revelation at the 1990 World Cup in Italy, in an England side that made the semis before bowing out to the Germans on penalties, the diminutive defender was no overnight success.

Having paid his dues at Fulham's Craven Cottage, his persistently high-class performances for neighbours Queens Park Rangers at centre-half and sweeper made him hot property by the time Alex Ferguson brought him in after securing the Cup Winners' Cup in 1991.

Unfortunately, injuries have played an ever-increasing part in the career of the speedy converted full-back, and, although Viv Anderson never enjoyed the honours Paul has in his spell at the club, their experiences are similar in that the long periods of frustration threaten to overshadow all the good times they were around for.

The Boss certainly caused a few raised eyebrows when pulling Parker off the treatment table to deputise for Steve Bruce in a man-marking role against Romario of Barcelona in the 1994/'95 edition of the Champions' League. The skipper took some pacifying before he was returned to the side for the away leg!

The emergence of the Nevilles will inevitably have some impact on a fully-fit Parker's prospects, but the 31-year-old will hopefully retain all the qualities that have made him a real one-off – he still made Terry Venables' first England team, against Demark – and be pushing the brothers all the way.

As a man-marker, Paul still has few peers in the European game.

PAUL PARKER
Defender

Birthplace:	West Ham
D.O.B:	4th April 1964
Height:	5'7"
Transferred from:	QPR 6.8.91
Previous Clubs:	Fulham, QPR
United Debut:	17.8.91 vs Notts County
Full International	England

PAUL PARKER
LEAGUE RECORD FOR UNITED

Season	Apps	Goals
1991-92	24(2)	0
1992-93	31	1
1993-94	39(1)	0
1994-95	1(1)	0
Total	95(4)	1

PAUL PARKER
INTERNATIONAL FOR ENGLAND

Debut:	26.7.89 vs Albania
Appearances	19
Goals	0

HE WILL HOPEFULLY RETAIN THE QUALITIES WHICH SAW HIM MAKE TERRY VENABLES' FIRST ENGLAND TEAM – AND PUSH THE NEVILLE BROTHERS ALL THE WAY

Manchester United

European Champion Clubs' Cup
Winners 1968

European Cup Winners' Cup
Winners 1991

FA Premiership
Champions 1993 1994
Runners-up 1995

Football League Division One
Champions 1908 1911 1952 1956 1956 1957 1965 1967
Runners-up 1947 1948 1949 1951 1959 1964 1968 1980 1988 1992

FA Challenge Cup
Winners 1909 1948 1963 1977 1983 1985 1990 1994
Finalists 1957 1958 1976 1979 1995

Football League Cup
Winners 1992
Finalists 1983 1991 1994

European Super Cup
Winners 1991

FA Charity Shield
Winners 1908 1911 1952 1956 1957 1983 1993 1994
Joint Holders 1965 1967 1977 1990

Manchester United Football Club plc
Old Trafford
Manchester
M16 ORA

Directors
CM Edwards (Chairman)
JM Edelson
Sir Bobby Charlton CBE
EM Watkins Ll.M
RL Olive
RP Launders

Chief Executive
Martin Edwards

Manager
Alex Ferguson CBE

Secretary
Kenneth Merrett